Churnings

Verse by Jim Gronvold

Also by Jim Gronvold

Back River

Oak Bones

Star Thistle

Pith & Piffle

Word and Mortar

Cogs Turning

Sphere Sun

Churnings

Verse by Jim Gronvold

Oak Ink Press 2022

Copyright © 2022 Jim Gronvold
All rights reserved

ISBN-13: 978-1-7362973-2-2

Book and cover design by Jeremy Thornton
Cover artwork by J. Alan Constant

To order additional copies
Or to contact the author, write:

OAK INK PRESS
oakinkpress@icloud.com
or visit
www.jimgronvold.com

*Dedicated to
Defenders
of Democracy*

Acknowledgements

With gratitude to *The Lyric* and *The Seventh Quarry,* in which the following poems first appeared:

The Lyric: Mulberry Smoke; Dots

The Seventh Quarry: Whorls; Updraft; Today; Dylan Thomas's Boathouse

Contents

I

Bang 3
Surge 4
Whorls 5
Guest 6
Vitality 7
Skin 8
Similar 9
Steps 10
Trick 11
Feeling 12
Beyond 13
Many 14
Adapting 16
Timing 17
Existential 18
Mix 19
Hope 20
Pieces 21
Dust 22
Desire 23
Sentence 24

Escape 25
Cracks 26
Grief 27
Stuck 28
Golden Rule 29
Fear 30
Mobs 31
Reverse 32
Forward 33
Plans 34
Synapse 35
Ration 36
Focus 37
Music 38
Art 39
Churnings 40
Hone 41

II

Coastal Dawn 45
South to San Francisco 46
Bridge Beat 47
Remind 48
Steam 49

March	50
Levee	51
Mulberry Smoke	52
Buckeye	53
Fan Palm	54
Limantour Road	55
Seashore	56
Snowy Plover	57
Bay Trail	58
Golden Gate Ferry	59
Whiff	60
Distant Shower	61
Dots	62
Swallows	63
Updraft	64
Dragonflies	65
Wingless	66
May Sky	67
Vista	68
Framed	69
Leaves	70
November	71
Twigs	72

Sun Skaters 73
Amber Air 74
Forecast 75
Ice Embers 76
Moon 77
Quiet 78
Sublime 79
Company 80

III

68th 85
70th 86
75th 87
Today 88
Chance 89
Reminders 90
Wiser 91
Delay 92
Aphorisms 93
Snout 94
Dylan Thomas's Boathouse .. 95
Dreams 96
Legacy 97
Life As Life 98

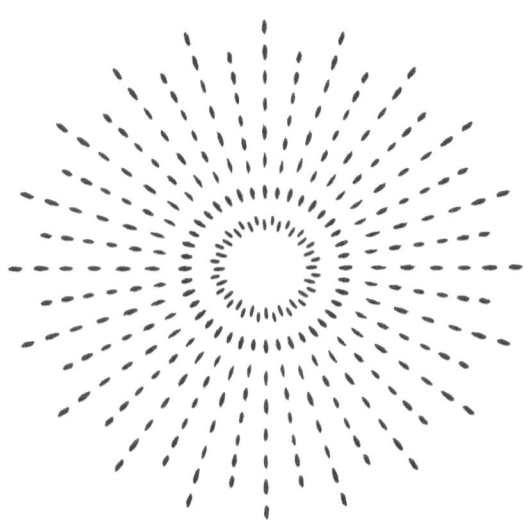

I

Bang

From the deepest
shadows of dark time

the fierce force
of first-source

caused an explosion
so intense and vast

that it splintered the void
with the ripples it cast

and still expands
the sparkling sands

of swirling stars
that sail between

the blast of All-birth
and the ever-unseen.

Surge

Water flows
and waves curl.

Grains of sand
roll with tides

or leap and fly
when dry winds swirl

around this rock
that spins and slides

through dark seas
that swell and churn

with spark stars
that time divides

to tiny dots
that glimmering glide

on undulations
that spreading turn

the galaxy
our moment rides.

Whorls

In fine, clear, moments
when heart and mind
align for a bright —
but brief — beat of time

sight and insight
might combine
in spinning currents
that read as rhyme.

Silent swirls
of elements
that flow from
roaring torrents

as waning whirls
of turbulence
that churning turn
through impermanence.

Guest

We belong to the sky
the earth and sea.

None of which wish
a minute with me

though I spend hours
in their company

and centuries as dust,
eventually.

Vitality

Spirit enough
in vitality.

The spark-stuff
of our energy.

The innate drive
to be alive.

The twinkle of eye
or smile in a sigh.

The breath held
to savor a moment

or breath expelled,
but not yet spent

until the last
must fade and die.

Skin

Human connections
allow us to see

our own reflections
in different skin.

Our own reactions
with a different spin

as kinship within
the diversity

of our planet's
many complexions.

Similar

This singular day
is like any other

in that they
do not return.

Some freeze, some burn,
some seem the same.

But each have patterns
they rearrange

within conditions
that constantly change.

Separate, yet alike.
Resembling or strange.

Mixtures of color
in shifting frames.

Similar textures
with different names.

Steps

What starts
will stop.

One step ends,
the next begins.

Each will rise.
Each will drop.

All are part
of a journey

of single steps
that living spins.

Trick

Time is a trick
that clocks tick—
a finite figment
of infinity.

Life too brief
despite belief
in a feeling
for eternity

but long enough—
smooth or rough—
to savor some
serenity.

Feeling

Air is the spirit
in choirs of leaves.

Love, the breath
of sweetness shared.

Time, a feeling
that—falling—grieves

all things passing
that can't be spared.

Beyond

In the harmony
of here and now

the divinity of
cause and effect

can be taught with
some certainty

of nothing certain
beyond the curtain

of the farthest stars
we have yet to detect

and the vast past
they must reflect.

Many

While humans exist,
I am not alone.

Breath of my breath.
Bone of my bone.

Though far apart,
we're one family

bound by the blood
of long history

with different ways
of expressing

the sorrows we bear
and loves we sing

in moments we share
or contemplate

as we interact
or isolate

with equal reason
to celebrate

until our time
reduces us

to ash of our ash,
and dust of our dust.

And we return
to soil, or float

on water or wind,
wave or gust

drifting through air
from flake to mote.

Flecks on a speck
of spinning crust.

Adapting

Shaped by seasons
and how we attune

to shifting sands,
for seas of reasons.

From lost ground
to wide horizons.

In fine weather
or shelter-bound

our hopes rise
as we find ways

to rewrite days
the times revise

again and unending
by repeat or surprise.

Timing

We advance at the pace
of our circumstance

to the tune and tone
of a halting dance

by the skill of our step
and the timing of chance.

Or circle ourselves
in our own shadow's trance

spinning to dust
in the starlit expanse.

Existential

It's not only
not to die.

It's also the way
that we survive.

It's the choices
we make

and chances
we take

to be alive —
in the wonder of why.

Mix

We're a mixed bag,
and better for it.

Posh or rag-tag,
strong or unfit.

The shy, the wag,
the bore or wit.

We all do better
when we share

more than mere
due respect

and don't expect
things to be perfect.

Hope

Wishes are water
that slips through fingers.

Longing is a sharp
ache that lingers.

Trust can be dreams
of innocence

and promises pester
the peace of patience.

But experience
nurtures common sense

and hope is the heart
of existence.

Pieces

Paradise is present —
in pieces — right here.

Bliss might take
some time to find

but bits of beauty
can be anywhere

that senses align
with an open mind

and slices of pleasure
are held with care

as chances change
or shift by degrees.

Heaven, a weather,
not always fair

but there in the moment
we stop to seize.

Dust

Lovers polish
the ash of stars.

The dust of heavens
kissed into rust.

Affection or lust,
a stroking of scars

seeking moments
that feelings might trust.

Heartbeat echoes
of blinking pulsars

their moment as true
as time is unjust.

Desire

Feelings don't
keep well on ice

or last for long
breathing fire.

A strong impulse
evades advice

in pursuit of
a heart's desire.

But frost or flame
entice a price

of consequence
that could be dire.

Sentence

Some wounds
seem to never heal

no matter how well
we think we feel.

They open again
on a memory

a phone call
or anniversary.

Just an old photo
or a melody

and the heartache
can feel as real

as a life sentence,
without appeal.

Escape

The escape we
swallow, or inhale,
might seem to fill
the cracks in a day

but buries
what's broken
in shallow graves
of time killed
avoiding problems
that won't go away.

And what began
as a distraction
comes to command
our full attention —
with loss but part
of the price we pay.

Cracks

The dread we deny
and don't address

collects concerns
we might not express.

But, worry, like water
off an iceberg's back

will find a fissure
and widen the crack.

Distress we conceal
or try to finesse

will leak at the seams
and burst, nonetheless.

Grief

However it happens,
it hurts when they leave.

Loss is loss
however we grieve.

And it's hard to see
an end to sorrow

when the future is not
what we may know.

But remember, today
is not tomorrow

and grief is a pain
that time can relieve

in ways that sadness
might not perceive.

Stuck

While we argue
over what is true

what's mine or yours,
or good or bad

and disagree
on what to do:

leaves drink light
and flowers glow

day and night
come and go

while we lose sight
of hopes we had

and cling to what
we thought we knew.

Golden Rule

Malignant mayhem
fills the airwaves
with daily news
of nightmares come true.

Corrupt politicians
fan popular fears,
inciting mobs
that take their bait.

Children, in turn,
are taught to hate
and suffer for lack
of a simple virtue.

Fear

As the world we know
seems to look strange

many feel threatened
and afraid of change.

Some, in anger,
might even join

liars who drum
the fear they sell

willing to war
and wage hell

for one side
of the same coin.

Mobs

Dark Age shadows
bark at our heels.

Menacing mobs
led by lies

threaten the progress
of centuries.

Tyrants steal
the sound of ideals

twisting the truth
until trust dies

and gangs terrorize
democracies

as conspiracies
spark atrocities.

Reverse

Time doesn't
move in reverse.

But we may dread
what lies ahead

and yearn for a past
that, in fact, was worse.

Worry rewrites
our memory.

We fret and forget
our history

and fear ignites
hostility

that repeats the
old insanity.

Forward

Not what was
or was to be

nor any dream
of days ideal.

No future facts
too soon to see

nor view of things
we knew or know

can answer now
what will be real

despite a wish
for tomorrow.

Plans

Take nothing,
or no one,
for granted.

All that is sure
is the odds
may be slanted

unfairly in favor
of fickle chance.

Or some aspect
one would not expect.

Some — game-change-
deal-break minor detail

that should raise red flags
where plans could fail

without sufficient
vigilance.

Synapse

In patterns between
body and mind

impulses weave
threaded lightning.

Hands hold thoughts
and hearts heave.

Feet find balance
and sight is refined

as senses send signals
back to the brain

to ascertain
pleasure or pain

all in the flash
of silent storms

that any shifting
second forms.

Ration

New life and loss
are everywhere

in this ration of days
that we burn through

as if we had more
than time would spare.

Though, to be fair,
each moment is new

but gone on a breath,
and time couldn't care.

Focus

When the dust settles
and thoughts clear

attention may turn
to fascination

and minutes so full
they disappear

in timeless hours
of concentration

as thought wheels turn
and find their gear.

Music

Sounds that express
thoughts that dare

to shape tones
that feelings share

unwind vibrations
with measured care

breathing the pulse
of rippled air

beating their time
into our bones

echoing rhythms
once pounded on stones.

Art

Heart is the core
of human care.

The thoughtful judge
of the true and fair.

Art is the skill
of mind and heart

to smartly distill
refined perception

of that of which
we are a part.

Churnings

As daylight and
darkness will return,
our inclinations
may chill or burn.

Accept or regret.
Yearn or spurn.
Forget or recall,
with luck we learn

that feelings change
as thoughts churn,
while shades of seasons
continue to turn.

Hone

Mortality sharpens
a quick mind

the way night sky
can clarify

deep questions
that mystify

as stars grind
into daylight

and sight anoints
the whetstone

that insights hone
to piercing points.

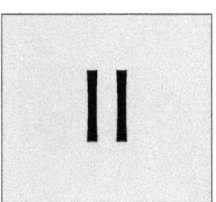

Coastal Dawn

Wake to the ocean
breaking white

on the shadowed shore
dripping light

off a cypress slope
and fir point forest

greening under
brightening blue.

And rise, at rest,
to the greeting sight

of the ocean's
splashing pulse.

Then button up,
tie each shoe

and open the door
to enter the view.

South to San Francisco

Hug the curve
to the tunnel.

Squeeze through
to the strait side

where bridge towers
raise their heads.

Then slide down
to the wide span

that swallows
the highway you fly

and glimpse the ivory city—
teeth bared to the blue sky.

Bridge Beat

Driving between
ocean and bay

open windows
catch the beat

of asphalt seams
thumping low

in tapping-time
to radio jazz

while breezes strum
steel cables

to the cool pitch
of a wind-reed hum

and wheels brush
the concrete drum

in surreal rhythm
on the golden span

between wild ocean
and Alcatraz.

Remind

I needn't tell the day that night
gives brilliance to its passing light.

Nor try to spell the skies I've seen.
Or dwell on what a cloud could mean.

Can't chirp as only birds can sing
to ring the leafy bell of Spring.

But must remind these busy days
how simple details still amaze.

Steam

Coffee outside
is Spring bliss
when sunlight
returns to
timid skin,
and time forgets
how to begin.

Tea indoors
by a window,
on a day as cold
as rain or snow,
is another kind
of calming kiss
that can warm
a winter oasis
and hush a wish
for days we miss.

March

Hopeful are days
of longer light

and nights full
of moon-bright.

An end to cold
come into sight

like dawn spun
from twilight.

Levee

Between this levee
and the nearest hill

in the wake of wind
no stalk stands still.

Streaming patterns
on the floodplain

tip whitecaps
of rolling grain

at the mercy of
wind's fickle will

while over the bay
breezes play

between warm air
and winter's chill.

Mulberry Smoke

Small puffs
of mulberry pollen
burst in the blink
of a bold wink

and disappear
in the crowd of leaves,
slick as smoke
and quick as thieves

trusting their luck—
on a breeze—
to find the flowers
of fertile trees.

Buckeye

The Buckeye blossoms
I breathe today

are a scent I'll forget
before next May

when they return
to this edge of the bay

like candles set
on a pollen buffet

only once a year—
to my regret.

But part of their charm
is in their delay.

Fan Palm

Few things rustle
like this palm
in the wind.

Its whisper
a tumbling
stream on fire.

Flailing fronds
rattle the air

and wrestle for breath
in a swaying choir

singing in tongues—
seeming to swear

under the weight
of the sky's desire.

Limantour Road

Mandolin pine-shadows
strum the windshield

winding through
the sun-stringed forest

to the cello deep valleys
of the violin crest

and a trumpeted view
of ocean, to the west.

Seashore

You might not
bask in the sun

take a picture
or dive in the sea.

You might just
stroll the sand

shed your shoes
to set toes free.

Or sit in sight
of a blue horizon

and drift the swells
of a fantasy.

Snowy Plover

Scamper…scamper…stop.
Dip..nip..and run.

Footprint too
fine to find.

Dun color of sand
in noon sun.

One tiny step ahead
of extinction.

Running from talons
and folks on vacation.

Bay Trail

Walking this path
past running grass

wind racing sunlight
sets fields a-shimmer.

Summer morning
soon to simmer

beside this bay
of rolling glass.

Golden Gate Ferry

Rising sky
on the big bay

a palette of blue,
white and gray

paints water folds
of cloud reflections

stippled with winking
gem refractions

that draw me into
a larger day.

Whiff

A breath of soil
on soft air

after a brief
summer rain

resurrects what
scents remain

of a long
forgotten feeling

in a memory
of ancient Spring.

Distant Shower

Below the shadow
of a distant cloud

sliding lines
shimmer in sunlight.

A silver-string rain-harp
plays the horizon

in far-off silence
heard only by sight

but felt in the deep
breath of this place

and the wide grace
of open space.

Dots

A tiny flutter
flickers on high.

A small white dot
on a pale sky.

If I were caught
in that bird's eye

it would be a spot
the Kite would spy.

Swallows

Swallows all over
this path by the bay

dip right and left
in the deft way

they make hunting look
like a game they play

swooping and looping
and slipping away

on the sundown slide
of a summer's day.

Updraft

Gulls air-surf
crushing curls

riding long moments
inches from edges
of stretches of swirls

scratching their
feather-tip shadows

on crashing crests
as ancient and fresh
as the ocean flows
and the planet twirls.

Dragonflies

Flying fossils
of glaze-lace wing.

Paleo-shadows
dash over ponds

seeming to sing,
but beating echoes

of floating chains
and armor plate.

Prowling pools
for prey or mate

their buzzing drum
a whistling spear

thrown for hundreds
of millions of years.

Wingless

Standing where ocean
is equal to sky

thoughts can soar,
but not too high

with feet too heavy
for arms to fly:

while tumbling clouds
summersault by.

May Sky

Filament fiddlehead clouds

fade at the tips of brilliant stems

on shallow heavens, now blue

in the shadow-tide

where galaxies hide

between sunrise and evening's hue

seeding the dark with sparkling gems

between ripples of spangled dew.

Vista

Sigh at the sight
of a breathtaking view

for the one you knew
who would feel it too.

For anyone who
felt as you do

and those who will,
long after you.

Framed

Changing colors
catch a quick eye

as shades shift
through crawling sunlight

or flash on waters
under white-capped sky.

Some slide downhill
as dew shadows dry

or hang from horizons
at the corners of sight

on highway galleries
of frames drifting by.

Leaves

Watching leaves
on any tree

imagine how
they came to be

and how they all
will fall someday.

Breathe the breath
that we borrow

from all the leaves
we'll never know

and consider how
we came to grow

and how, in time,
we fall away.

November

November's lingering leaves
hang on as long as they can

surviving their season's span
while the naked forest grieves.

Not long ago buds were bursting
on a warming breeze of Spring

when everything green and fair
would seem to last forever.

But now their grip will waver
and stumble on icy air.

Twigs

Easy to see
sadness in trees

stark to the bark
without their leaves.

But trust life
to find a way

through every turn
that time weaves

and know that twigs
will bud again

when Spring returns
and Winter leaves.

Sun Skaters

Following fog,
burned off by noon

a twitching mist
on this leaf-bear hill

fills bright shafts
of winter light

with sun-skaters
spinning in flight —

a twirling dance
of winter gnats —

flashing en masse
in a mating throng

with too little time
to woo, for long

before those cracks
in the shadows pass.

Amber Air

Wild fire winds
spit the smoke

of plastic siding
and ancient oak

that paints the sky
and taints the lung

as we, our fields,
and songbirds choke

on the fumes
our choices stoke.

Forecast

Waters will rise
as oceans warm.

Crops will die
as dark skies storm.

Repeated drought
and industry

threaten the planet
and poison our health

but we still burn
the Earth's wealth

feeding the flames
of catastrophe

with dwindling
sources of energy.

Ice Embers

From this hill above
the tidal wetland

moon-burn
ice embers glow

through frozen shards
on the far edge

of the silver river
elbow below

cracking its knuckles
around the bend

as the marsh crawls
under a down of snow.

Moon

That sphere
worn round

grinding through
the shoreless sea

of space unwinding
the dream we wound

against the turn
of eternity.

Our tides tied
to its gravity

we tumble together,
slowly, around

an edge of our
drifting galaxy —

moonlight gently
dripping aground.

Quiet

To listen to trees, as they sway,
and not need to say how they sound.

Or watch waves rolling aground
and not be drowned by wordplay.

To float on an evening breeze
and not feel bound—in any way—

to expound on the end of the day,
or some insight I may have found.

Sublime

Wise to be still
and reconnect

to the wild depth
of natural beauty

and find harmony
in cause-and-effect

spun and sung
from sky to sea

through the soil
of intellect

to moments
of tranquility.

Company

This morning a wren
hopped past my cup

to the deer skull
on the hillside wall.

Later, while reading,
I looked up to see

two curious fawns
staring right at me.

But they were a bit
too shy to chat

and when greeted
were quick to flee.

Just after that
a Jackrabbit sat

in the birdbath
by the cedar tree.

Visits like these
make this place

my favorite spot
for company:

other than that
of the human race.

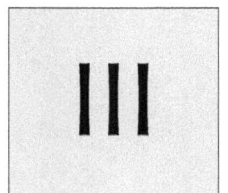

68th

This day is
a sweet reminder

that every day
a sky is born

as young as seasons
older than stone.

As fresh as sunlight
newly worn.

And old as a minute
about to be known.

70th

A day as light
as melting air

and fragrant as
dripping earth

refreshed by
overnight rain.

A day to consider
the distance

from birth to what
might remain.

75th

The Moon at the turning
of my bending age

burned a blue hole
in the midnight sky.

A pale blind eye
still staring

when waking sun
lit western hills

and the wicking moon
in mute reply

held my candle
not quite as high.

Today

Some days sparkle
from dew to dusk.

Others drag hours
through shadow or dust.

This day may flower
or hide in its husk.

But my day will find
the sunlight it must.

Chance

By chance of birth
and circumstance

we find or lose
our balance

with each new
step we take.

Each good or bad
choice we make.

Win or lose,
in the end

each deep breath
is a lucky break.

Reminders

Some things we said
in our youth
could bring us closer
to our truth

reminding us
that what we knew—
or thought we did—
might not be true

although the way
they made us feel
might stay with us
and seem as real.

Wiser

I have felt
"Forever"
in an hour

and "Never-again"
in the stroke
of a pen.

But "maybe"
is a promise
wiser than "when"

and "here" is where
prediction should end.

Delay

*"Tomorrow will
be another day."*

A common excuse
and old cliché.

But time has a way
of running away

and patience is
often little more

than how we delay
what we'd rather ignore.

Aphorisms

Sayings spun
off a clever pun

might sound right
for the moment

but lose their bite
in the spotlight

of logic or
legal argument

when wit or writ
sit in judgement

and sunlight
is abundant.

Snout

It's the job of poets
to nose about.

Sniff the breeze
for subtleties.

Snuffle through leaves
with a smart snout

and turn up words
that root out

a tasty phrase
that might please

or at least excite
an appetite.

Dylan Thomas's Boathouse

That close to the edge,
no dreams were small

but could rise and fall
on tides of sky

shifting the poet's
home on the hill

now silent as stars
or shouted by gulls

reciting flights
of wing-beat words

that once filled eyes
long since wept dry

as warned by seabird's
prophetic cries.

Dreams

In space between spaces
where mysteries flow

darkness embraces
hollow shadow.

Dreams change faces
and places we know

while sleep erases
worries we borrow

though some leave traces
too deep to forego.

Legacy

In sleep, I've seen
the silence
of those once here—
now history.

Awake, I've dreamt
their presence,
held somewhere
in my memory

and begun to see
that I carry them
the way that others
could carry me.

Which I take to mean
that we bear a share
of each other's
lingering legacy.

Life As Life

It's consciousness
that I venerate

and existence
that I celebrate.

Life as life,
and not some test

rewarded by
eternal rest.

Not part of a plan,
or a steppingstone

to a better place
in the dark unknown.

But life as a life
not spent in vain

but held as that
which can't remain.

www.ingramcontent.com/pod-product-compliance
Lightning Source LLC
Chambersburg PA
CBHW030042100526
44590CB00011B/298